The Peace of Me

By: Andrea Kasper

Illustrations and cover by Madison Telles

Andrea Kasper/The Peace of Me

Printed in the United States of America

Artwork by Madison Telles

Published by Cabeca Grove, Maryland USA

The Peace of Me/Andrea Kasper –1st ed.

ISBN 978-0-692-95964-0 Print Edition

*Disclaimer: In proceeding to the following pages and utilizing the activities in this book, the user acknowledges the writer and the publisher are not liable for any negative psychological outcomes. This journal is not intended to replace professional help or treatment. If serious psychological conditions are present, such as thoughts of self-harm or harm to others, or severe psychological distress, always consult a professional.

Table of Contents

For Caden, Caroline, and Benjamin

Introduction

I once was told by a psychiatrist friend that writing your thoughts can at times be as effective as professional counseling. This made sense to me as I had a journal, and found it very helpful.

As someone who tends to use the quiet of bedtime to reflect on the next day's needs and challenges, I found myself not always able to sleep well. As time went on and ideas became increasingly complex, I began to journal, and discovered that writing was really helpful for sleep. I realized that journaling was a great tool to see what I could or could not control and manage. I was able to integrate my feelings, identify issues at hand, and brainstorm to solve them. It was a wonderful way to clear my thoughts!

I have three children, and like many kids today, they face a lot of pressures as they navigate their way through friends, school, and growing up. They have busy minds like me, and find that bedtime brings the day's events to the forefront of their thoughts. I began to journal with them, to help them be in charge of their feelings.

At first, I had them speak their thoughts, and I wrote down everything that was on their mind. We then looked at what was written and began a discussion. This was great! I could have quality time with my children, while at the same time help them to process what was on their mind.

Because they are busy thinkers however, it wasn't always enough. We added different elements to the journaling so they could feel more in control of their lives and thoughts. For my son, figuring out what was in his control and what was not, was calming for him. What steps could he take to keep things on track? What could he let go of and how?

I also discovered that what worked for my son was completely different than what worked for my daughter. He had a whirlwind of thoughts moving through his mind, whereas she did not. He needed to write his thoughts down, and have space to explore them. In addition to writing down her thoughts, my daughter needed blank space to draw her days and emotions in order to process and unwind.

That's how The Peace of Me was created. It opens the piece of you that wonders or worries, that needs to be explored to relax the body and mind. Whether you both are using this journal to center the busy mind or explore feelings, these exercises can help your child better understand themselves. It can also teach them how to relax and create a calm, positive mindset. We all have challenges we face in life. Children especially though might not know how to navigate their thoughts, both good and bad, effectively. Journaling doesn't need to be done at bedtime; it can be done at any time to calm the mind. The Peace of Me offers an opportunity to have guided questions, and responses that can invite conversation, organization, and thoughtful processes. It's important to share with your child that there is absolutely *no judgement!* This journal is a *safe space* for their thoughts and ideas to foster a positive, resilient and healthy mind.

The guided questions are an invitation to explore. I suggest you try all of them with your child *and take as much time as you both need.* This journal has questions for the parents, as well, to enhance the conversation. I sit with my child one-on-one, and write for them as they speak, as they are still pretty young, and one of them does not enjoy writing. I encourage you to do what works well for you and your child. Try different times, and vary how often you would like to journal with your child to see what works best. Each family is different, and I will simply recommend you make sure it is never a "chore" for either one of you to do. You will also find an appendix in the back of the book for some suggestions, if needed.

The second half of the journal is meant to be more flexible. It's using what questions your child found helpful in the first part, and placing them in the second part, tailoring it to their benefit. Please feel free to add any questions or ideas of your own, and tailor these exercises to meet your child's needs. The intention is to help them to relax, discuss and move forward with their life more positively.

All of my children have found their journals helpful, and I hope it is for you and your children as well.

Enjoy!

Getting Started

1. Choose a time for both of you to sit down together and begin the questions. What works best? Day or night? How often during the week?

2. Decide ahead of time who will do the writing. Will it be the parent, child, or both?

3. Do you have a special pen that you'd like to use?

4. Some families might enjoy a visual when processing and writing, such as a chart to help explore their feelings. Find the appendix in the back of the book for examples and other suggestions.

Part One

What thoughts are going through your mind right now?

When finished, take three to five deep breaths.

For any thoughts that are unfavorable (thoughts that you don't like): Which ones do you have control over in your life? Which ones do you not have control over? Please write them below, and feel free to use the appendix if you need a chart suggestion:

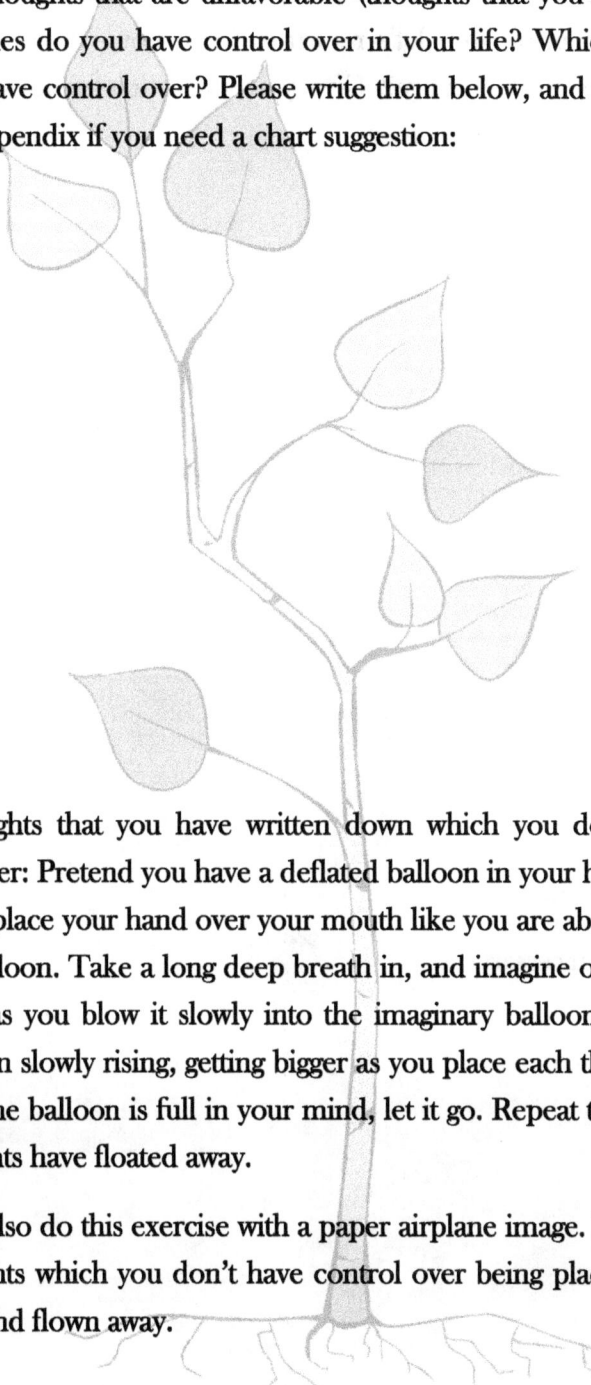

The thoughts that you have written down which you do not have control over: Pretend you have a deflated balloon in your hand. Make a fist and place your hand over your mouth like you are about to blow up the balloon. Take a long deep breath in, and imagine one of these thoughts as you blow it slowly into the imaginary balloon. Think of the balloon slowly rising, getting bigger as you place each thought into it. Once the balloon is full in your mind, let it go. Repeat this until all the thoughts have floated away.

You can also do this exercise with a paper airplane image. Imagine all the thoughts which you don't have control over being placed into an airplane and flown away.

If you have written down unfavorable thoughts in areas which you DO have control over, let's return to them now. What actions can you take to create change? Give yourself a timeframe to try these actions, and write down target dates.

Thought:

Action:

Time-frame for change:

(Repeat as necessary)

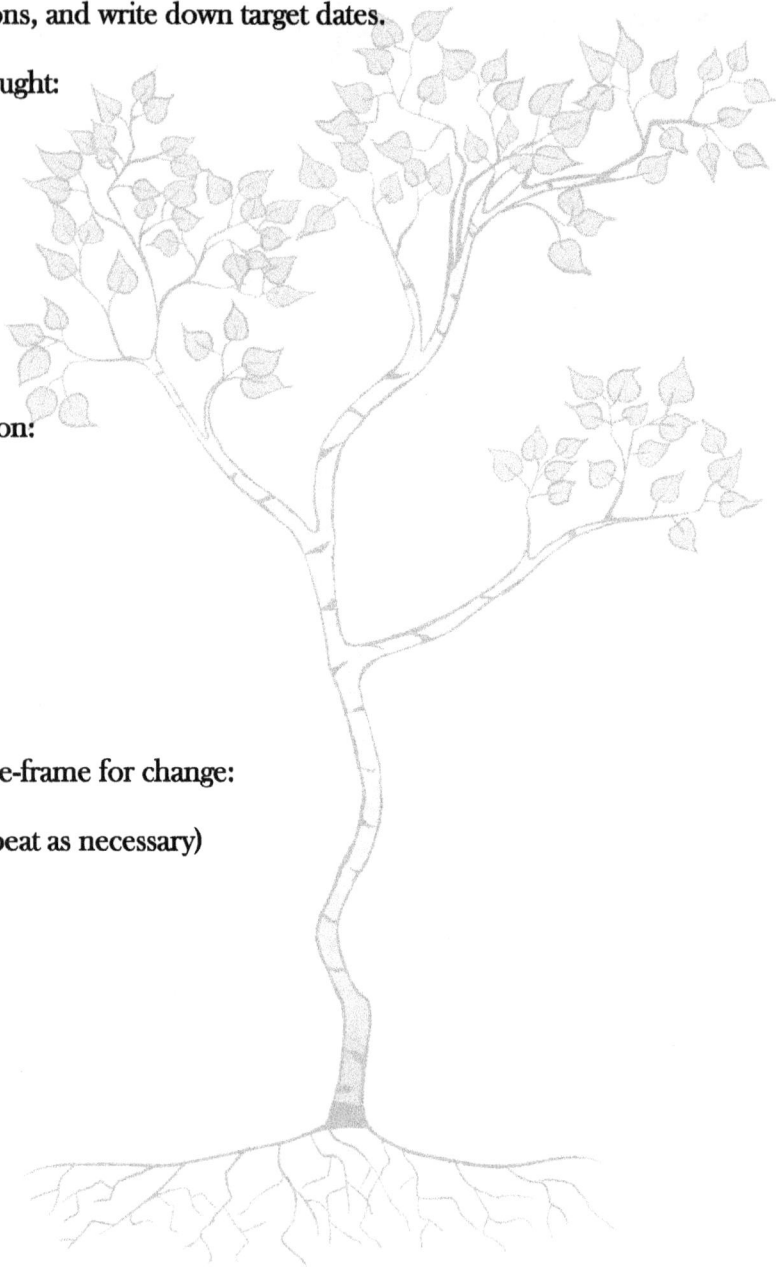

Child: Can you name some ideas that will help your body/mind relax?

What could be happening in your day when you'd want to use your above ideas to be more relaxed?

Parent: What are some other ideas that you can add to the list? Feel free to use the appendix if ideas are needed.

Breathe

Child: Name at least three things or qualities that are your strengths: (Hint: Think about who you are, not what you have)

Parent: What do you think your child's strengths are? Can you name at least three? Feel free to use appendix in back if ideas are needed.

Child: A hero is someone that you look up to and admire for who they are or what they've done. They could be someone you know, someone you've learned about in school or from a movie, the possibilities are endless. Who are your heroes? Can you name at least three?

What do you like about them?

Is there a quality in these heroes that you can see in yourself? What is it?

Parent: Who are your heroes? What do you like about them?

Can you name at least three? Feel free to use the appendix if ideas are needed.

Child: What are you grateful for? You can list anything; the big things and the little things, they all matter:

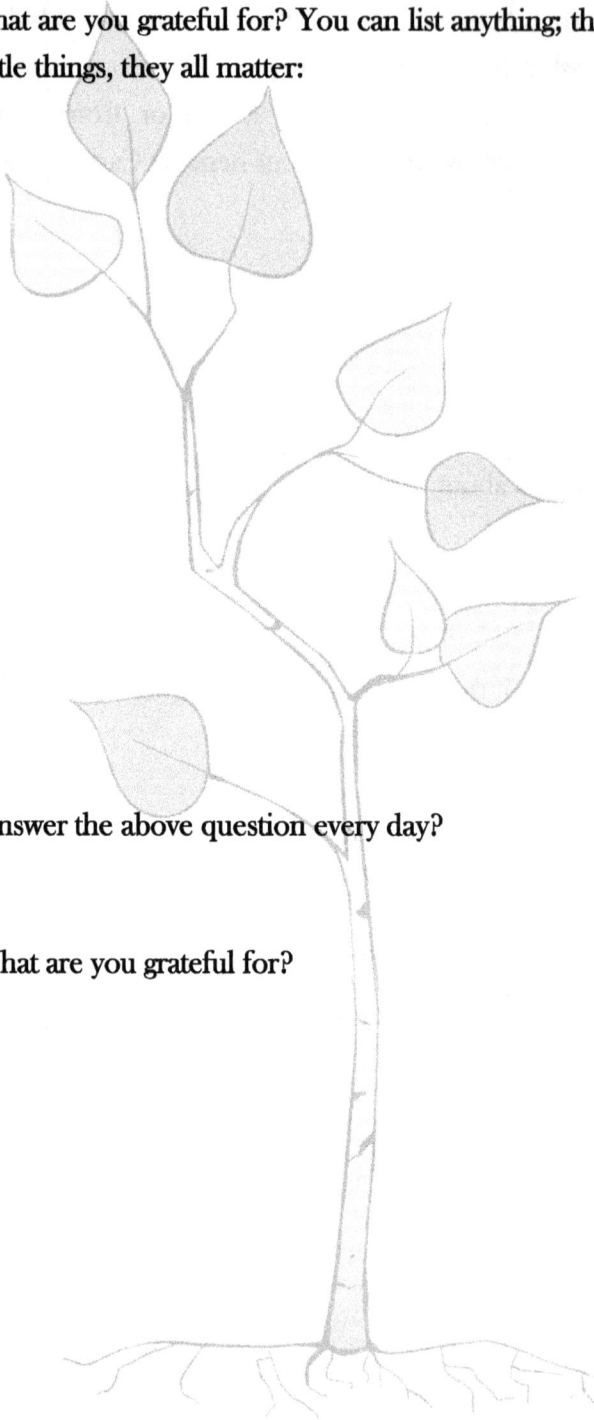

Can you answer the above question every day?

Parent: What are you grateful for?

Child: Can you name something that you did well today?

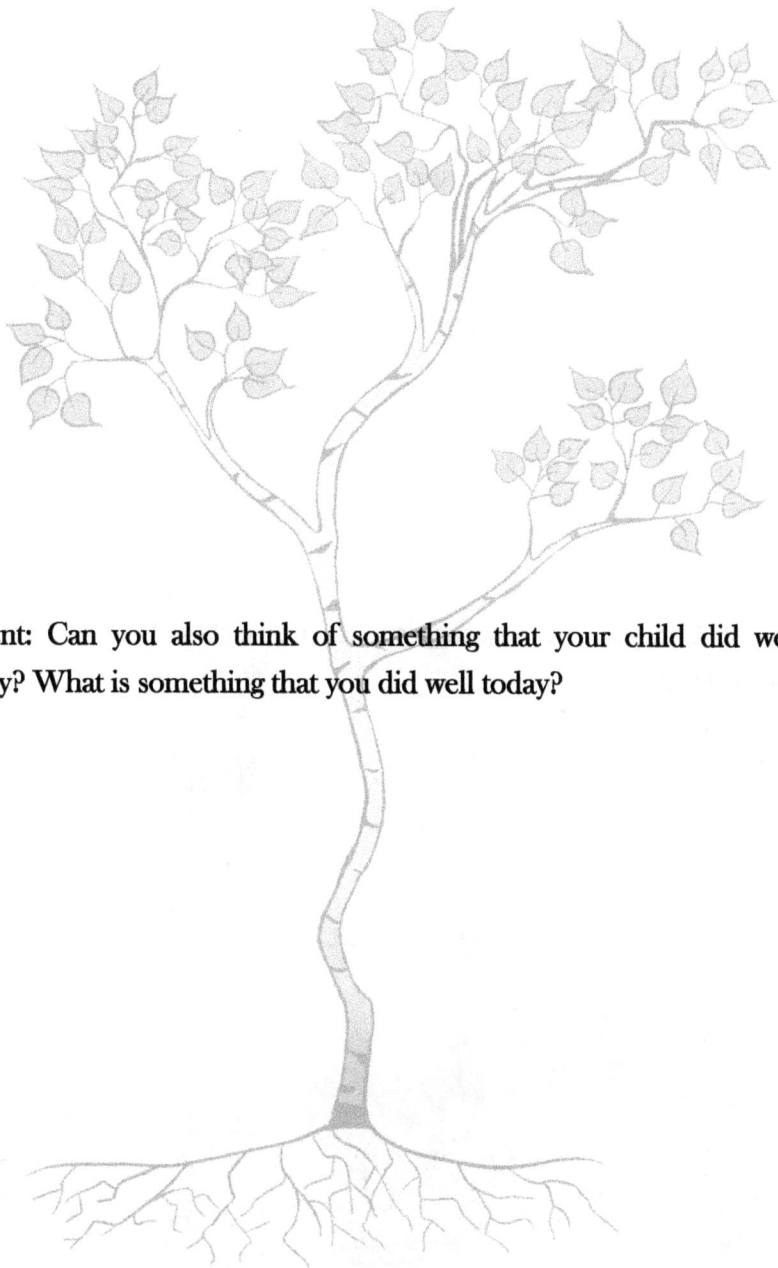

Parent: Can you also think of something that your child did well today? What is something that you did well today?

Child: What are you looking forward to?

Parent: Can you add any suggestions to this? What are you looking forward to?

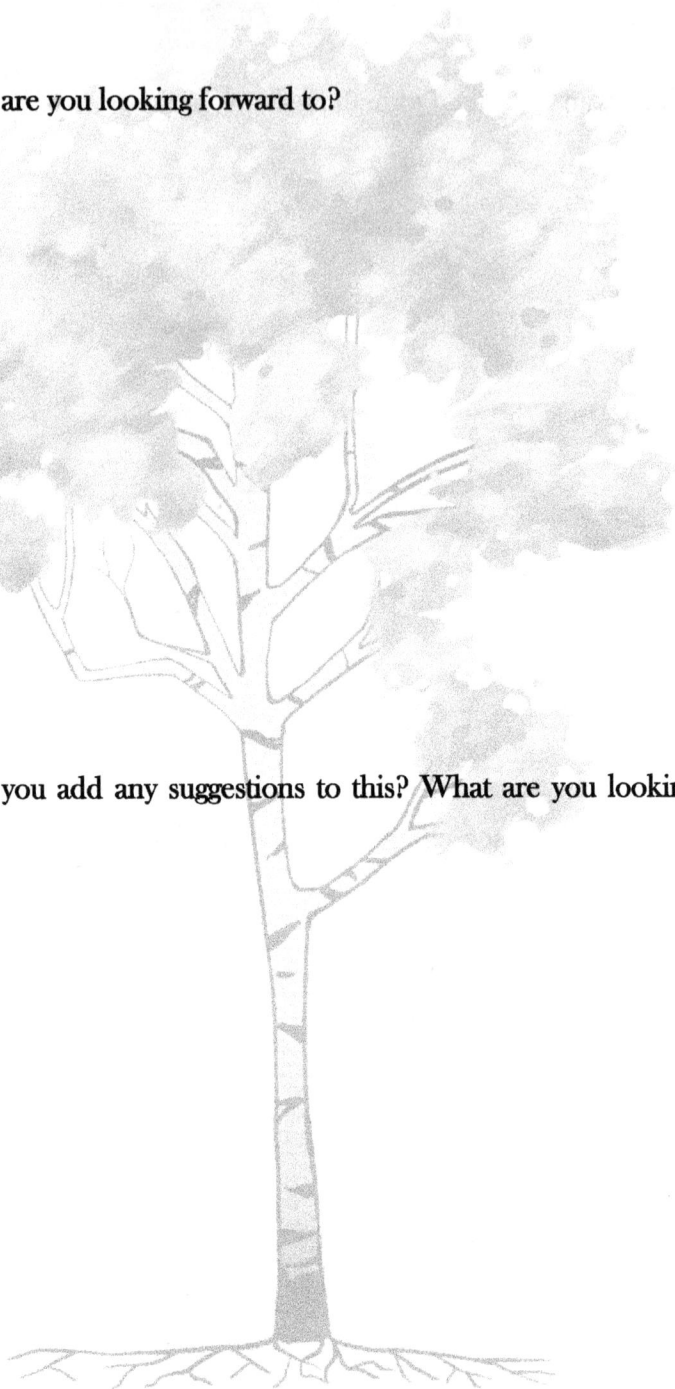

Child: What are the things you do in life that make you feel powerful, or good about yourself?

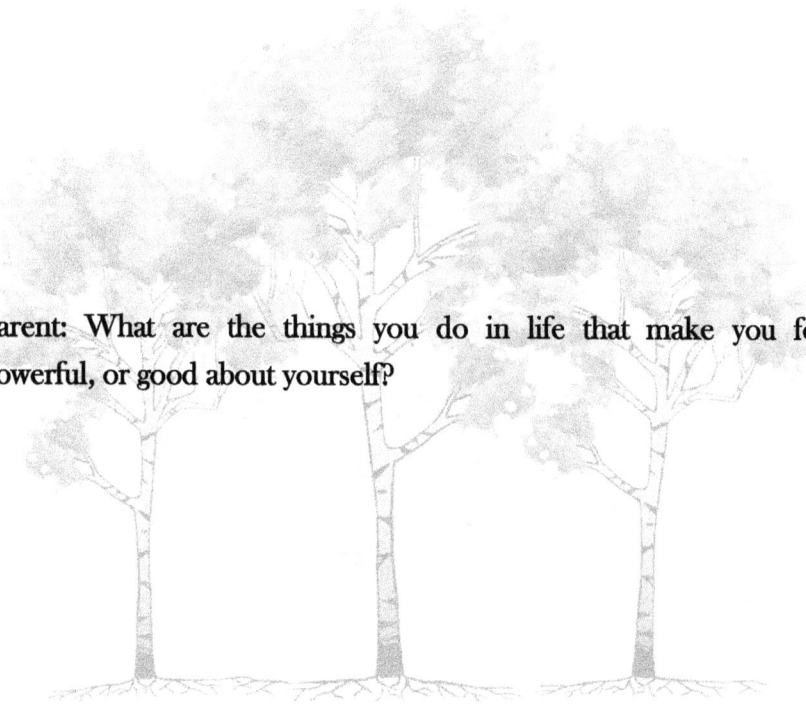

Parent: What are the things you do in life that make you feel powerful, or good about yourself?

Child: What do you enjoy doing or thinking about that makes you lose track of time?

Why?

Parent: What do you enjoy doing or thinking about that makes you lose track of time?

Why?

Child: Can you name three good things that happened today?

1.

2.

3.

What was the best thing that happened to you today?

Parent: Can think of three other good things to add to your child's list?

Please list three good things that happened to you today.

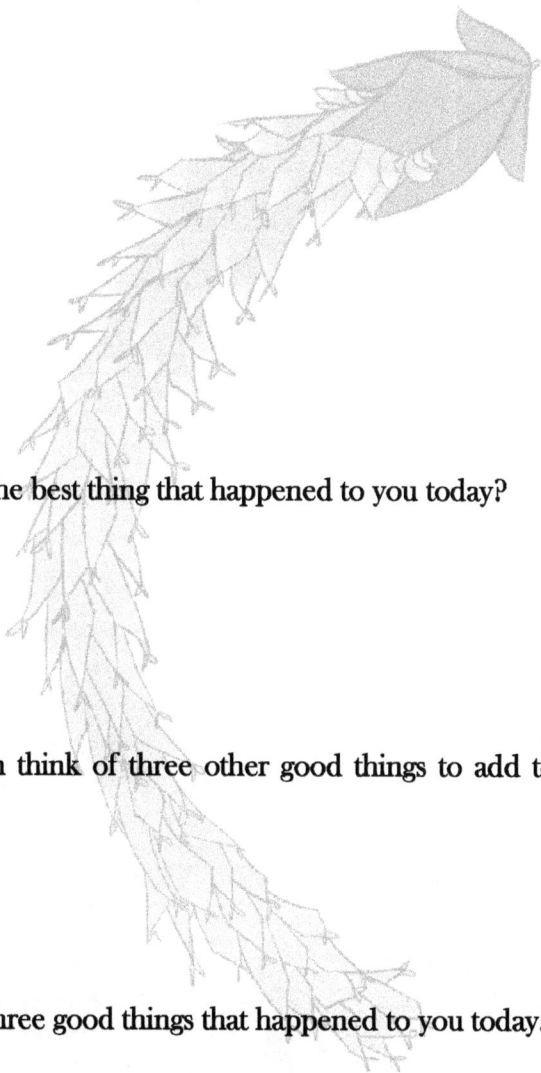

Use this space to write down some of your favorite positive words. If you don't have any yet, use this space to think of some. Fill the whole page if you can:

Child: Name a challenge or problem that you've solved in the past. What did you do to solve it?

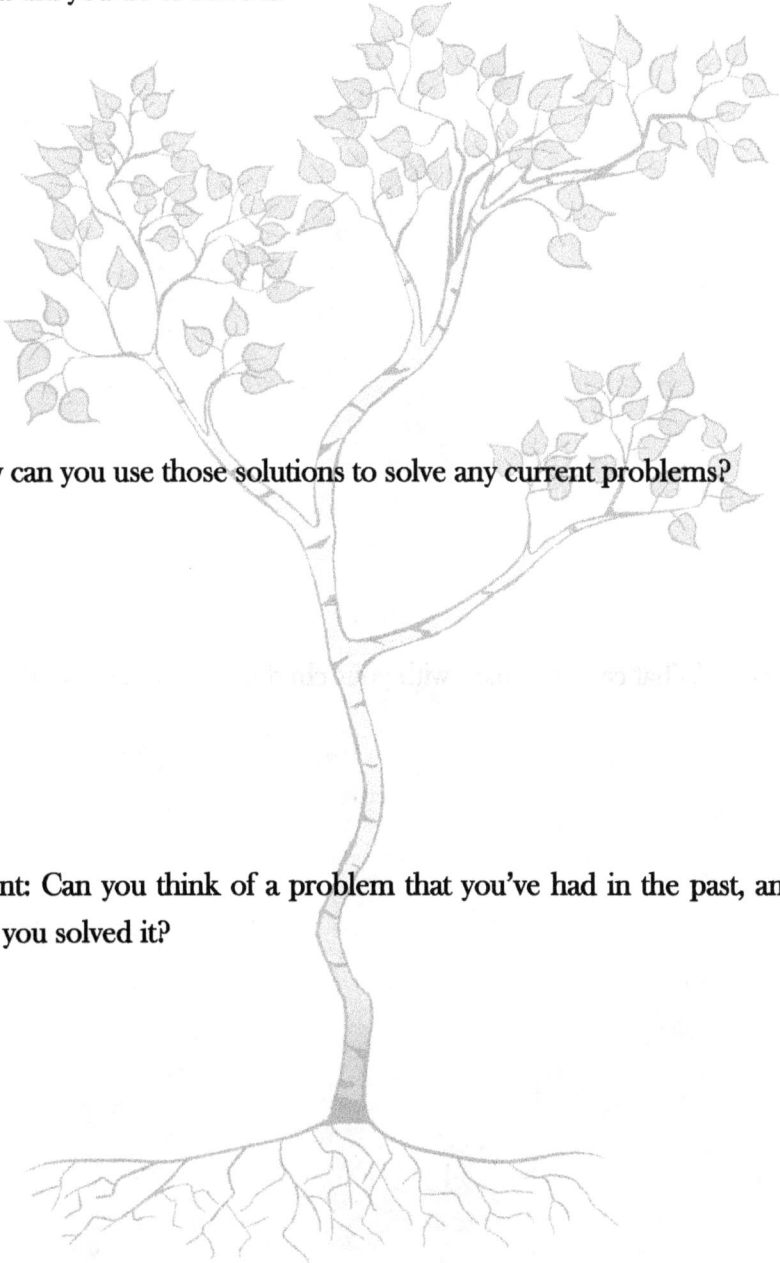

How can you use those solutions to solve any current problems?

Parent: Can you think of a problem that you've had in the past, and how you solved it?

Child: What could you say to yourself that would help a problematic situation?

Parent: What can you share with your child that would add to this?

Sometimes we can think something is happening as fact, when there's a different way to see it or think about it. This is known as perception. For example, imagine a student is misbehaving at school. One person's perception is that he/she is a "acting like a bad person." Another way to look at it though, is the "bad person" is someone who's struggling in some way perhaps personally or emotionally. The "bad person" is perceived as the "student who needs help." It's the same situation, but there are two different perceptions. Is there something happening in your life that could be perceived in a new light or thought of in a different way?

Child: Mistakes will happen in life. And they can be good for us because they teach us about life and help us grow. Can you think of a mistake that you've made in the past?

What can you learn from it?

Parent: Can you think of a mistake you've made in the past that helped you learn?

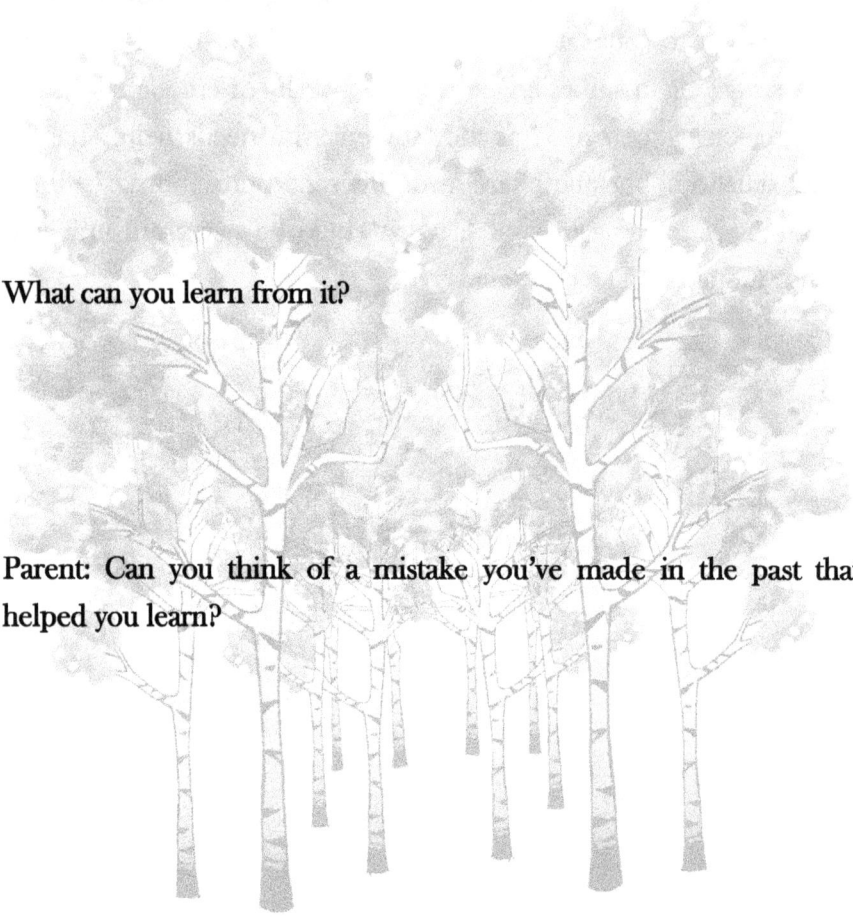

Child: If you could pick any goal for yourself, big or small, what would it be?

Can you think of a daily goal for yourself? Weekly? Monthly?

Parent: If you could pick a goal for yourself what would it be?

23   *Breathe*

Child: Have you ever wanted to say something to someone but didn't? What would you say? Use this space to say it here:

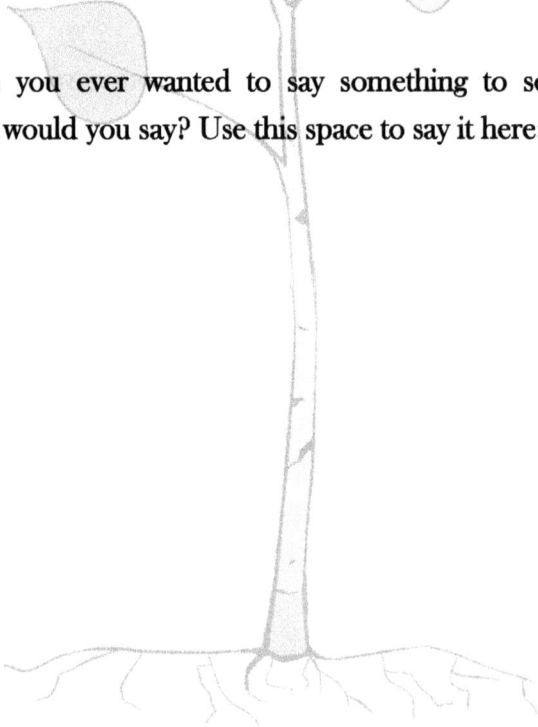

Parent: Have you ever wanted to say something to someone but didn't? What would you say? Use this space to say it here:

Child: If you could go anywhere, where would you go? Would you go alone or bring someone?

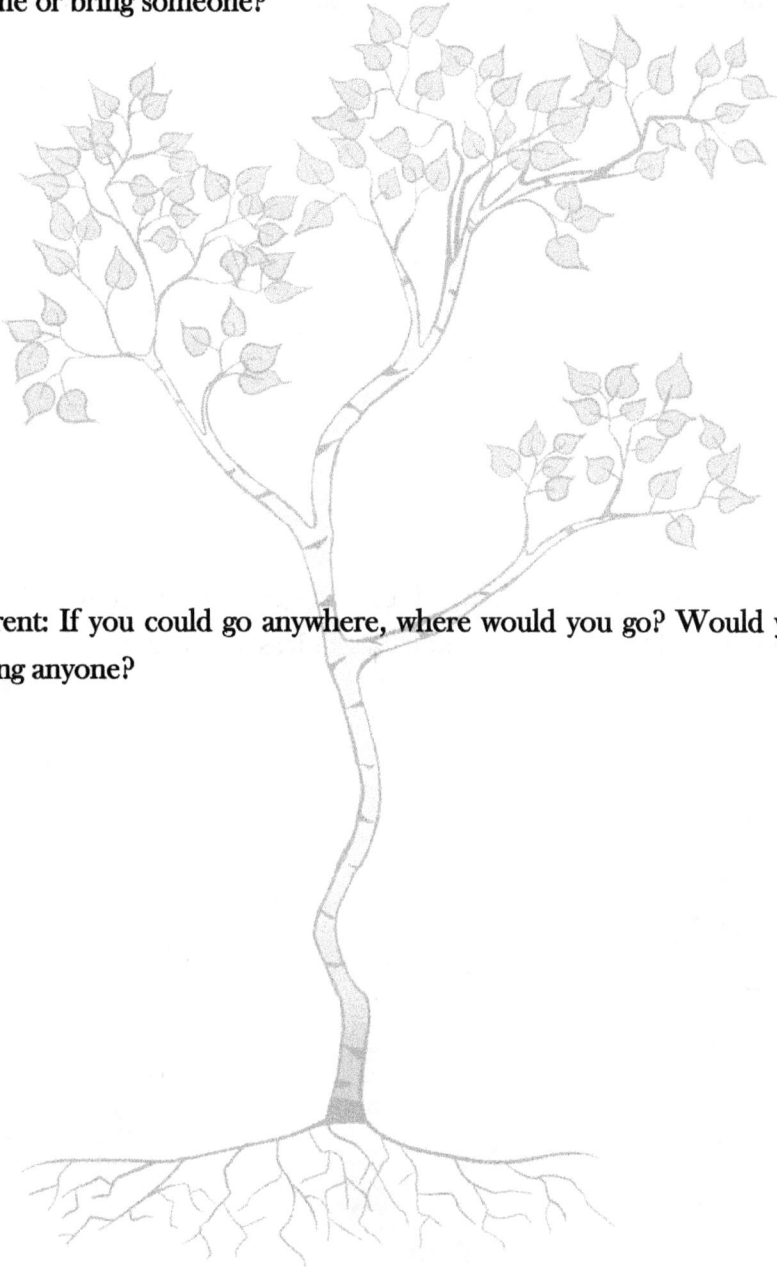

Parent: If you could go anywhere, where would you go? Would you bring anyone?

25

Child: If you could choose what to do for "Special Time" with your parent, meaning time spent with just the two of you, what would you pick?

Parent: What do you think of this suggestion? What would you choose? Feel free to use the appendix if ideas are needed.

Child: What are some of the greatest accomplishments (things that you've done) in your life so far? What other things would you like to do?

Parent: What are some of the greatest accomplishments in your life so far? What else would you like to achieve?

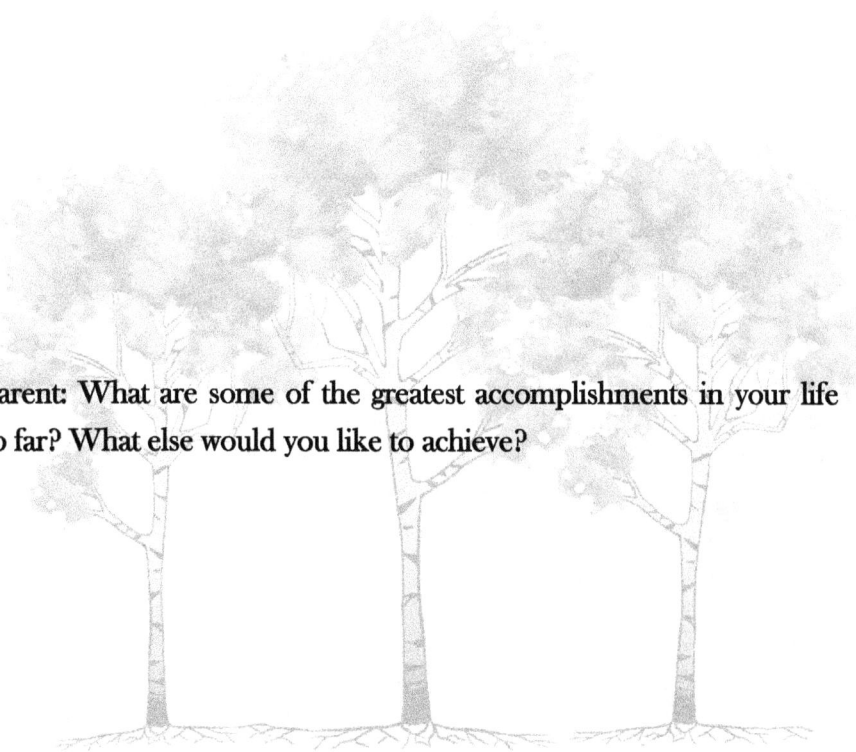

Child: What are the things in life that make you the most happy?
Make a list if you'd like:

Parent: What are the things in life that make you the most happy?

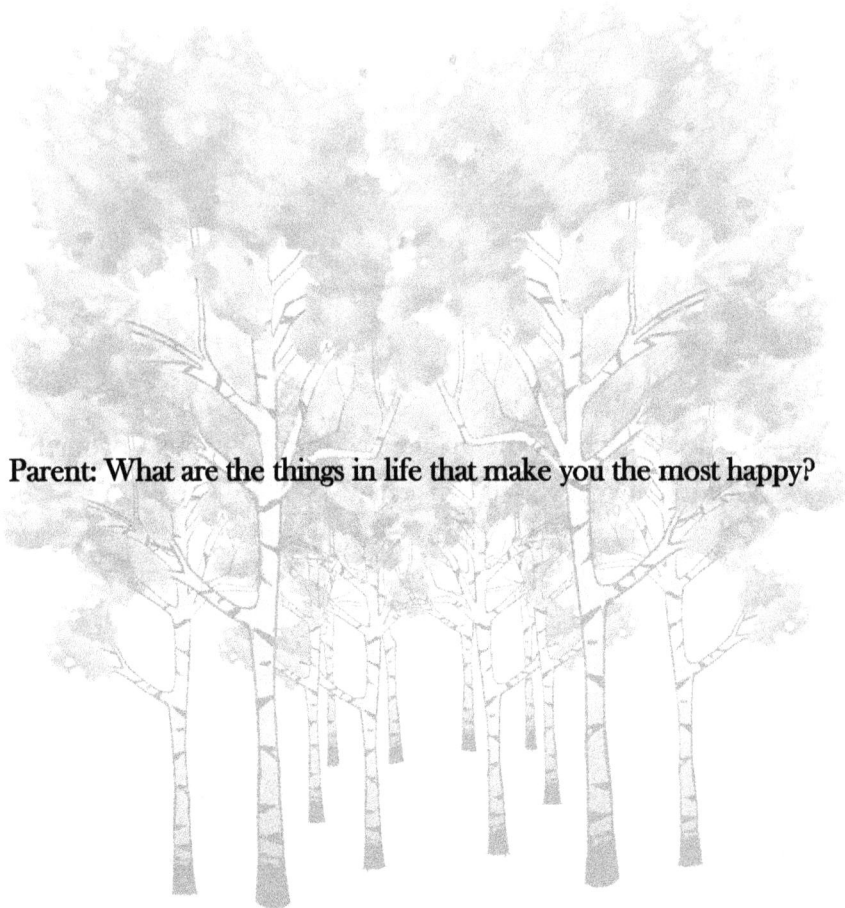

Draw a picture of your happy place:

Breathe

Child: What is something you'd like your parent to know about you?

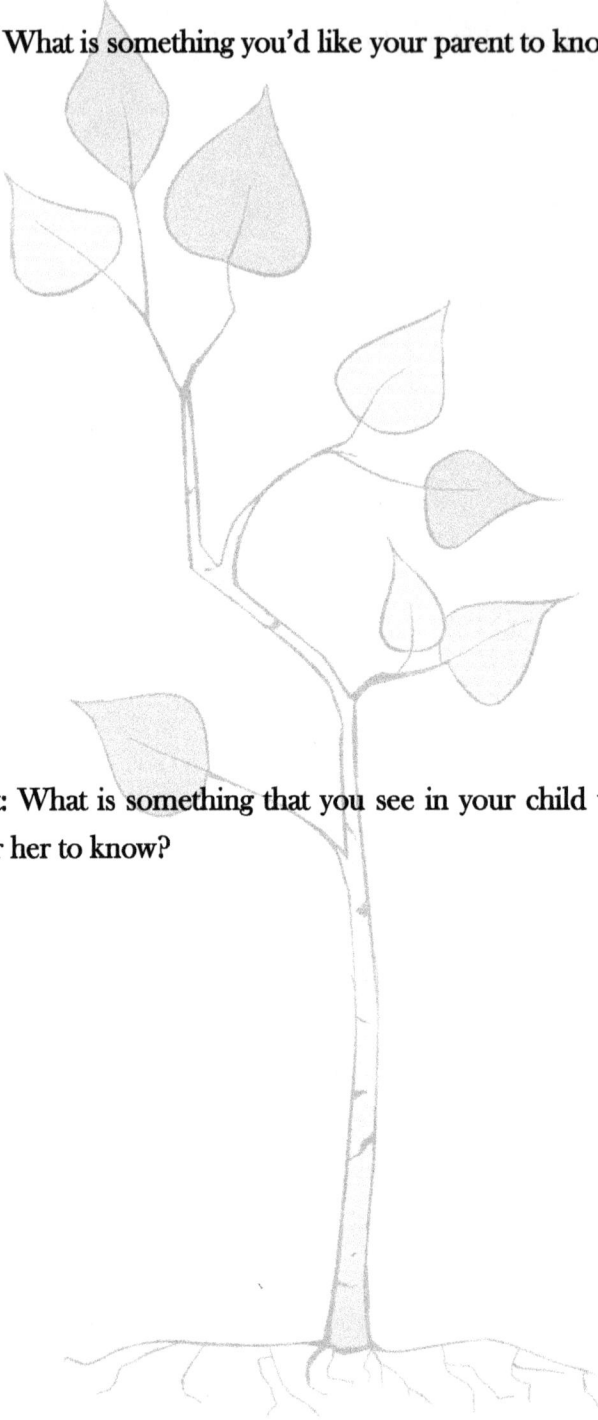

Parent: What is something that you see in your child that you'd like him or her to know?

Child: If you could change or add one thing about your life, what would it be?

Parent: If you could change or add one thing about your life, what would it be?

31   *Breathe*

Child: Name something that you could do or plan for today, which would set you up for a better tomorrow?

Parent: Name something that you could do or plan for today, which would set you up for a better tomorrow?

Child: What can you do to be brave today/tomorrow? It can be big or small.

How can you reward yourself for this action?

Parent: Can you add any ideas to this?

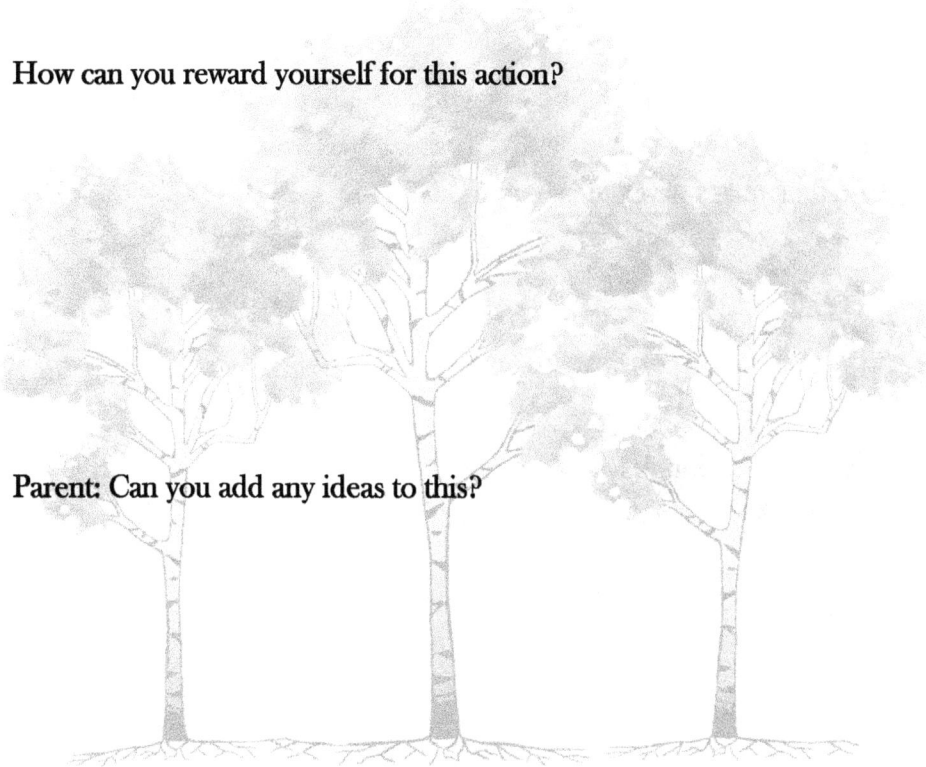

Child: What was the last dream you remember?

Sometimes dreams can be a way for our minds to figure out what is happening for us when we're awake. Does your dream sound like anything that's happening in your life? How so?

Parent: Do you have ideas about what your child's dream could mean? What was your last dream?

Child: If you could wish for something, what would it be?

Parent: What would your wish be?

Inspiration Page:

Use this space to cut out pictures from a magazine that you like, and paste them here to make a collage. You can also draw them if you'd rather not cut and paste.

Inspiration Page:

Drawing Page:

Breathe   38

Drawing Page:

The Story of Me:

The Story of You (According to your parent):

Breathe

Thoughts:

Thoughts:

Breathe

Thoughts:

Thoughts:

Thoughts:

Thoughts:

Breathe

Thoughts:

Thoughts:

Thoughts:

Thoughts:

Breathe

Thoughts:

Thoughts:

Breathe

Thoughts:

Thoughts:

Thoughts:

Part Two

Part Two:

This is the part that can be tailored just for you! Parents, use the questions from Part One that you enjoyed, or found helpful to relax and organize your child's thoughts. This is an opportunity to ask your child to pick questions that he/she would like to choose as well. Hopefully, in the first section, you both found questions that helped you understand each other and yourselves better. That's really important! You can even add in your own ideas or questions. Friend problems, sibling problems, homework, sports, it can get to be a lot. Again, this is a safe space with no judgement to write down thoughts and ideas. As always, I encourage you to start with what's on your child's mind. Remember to take deep breaths as you write and discover.

Breathe

Breathe

Breathe

Breathe

Breathe

Breathe

Breathe

Breathe

75

Breathe

Breathe

Breathe

81   *Breathe*

Breathe

Breathe

Breathe

89

Breathe

Breathe

Breathe

Breathe

Appendix

Suggestions to help relax:

Tense and relax muscles   Paint

Breathe Mindfully   Stretch

Bathe   Hug a pillow

Be in nature   Write

Listen to music   Massage

Suggestions for strengths:

Creative	Intelligent	Determined	Brave
Motivated	Thoughtful	Flexible	Imaginative
Athletic	Funny	Artistic	Friendly
Nice	Helpful	Adventurous	Curious

Suggestions for heroes:

Family	Yourself
Superhero	Firefighter
Teacher	Friend

Suggestions for special time:

Go out to breakfast	Scavenger hunt
Take a walk	Bake
Play a board game together	Indoor/outdoor picnic

Types of charts or graphs:

Some of the questions might be better broken out into a chart to see or understand your answer better. For example, the question that asks things that you have control over and don't might be better organized with a t-chart or a pie graph.

Control   Can't control

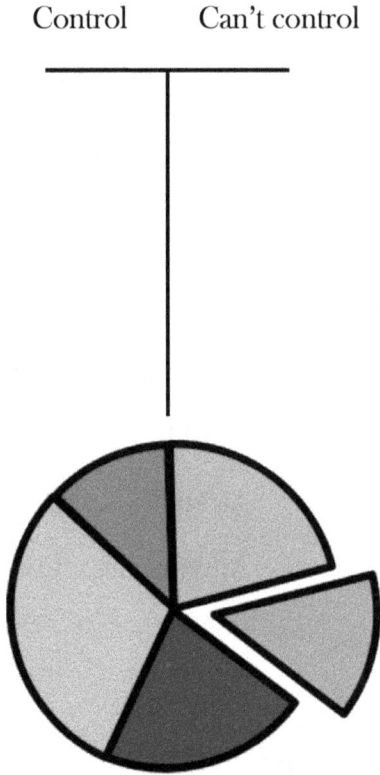